Welcome to Finland!

The Funniest F*cking Country in the World!

A. J. Ahola

Best Day Publishing
2024

Disclaimer: This book contains swearing and obscene words in English as well as Finnish. This book is intended for readers aged 18 and older.

Best Day Publishing
Annapolis, Maryland
AJAholaAuthor@gmail.com

ISBN 979-8-9917850-0-6

Table of Contents

Welcome to Finland!

Finland – the small country nestled in Northern Europe, that has managed to rise to the top of the world in just about everything important. They seem to excel effortlessly at the most important benchmarks of modern society such as health, happiness, and education, not to mention being identified as one of the safest countries on the planet. Additionally, Finns are renowned for being global leaders in environmental sustainability as well as gender equality. All very impressive indeed, but what you may not have heard about this reindeer-loving, sauna bathing nation, is that they may also be *the* funniest country known to mankind.

With their dry wit and slightly dirty minds, there is an undercurrent of seriously funny stuff running through this culture. It has been cultivated and nurtured for generations and has likely gone completely unnoticed by the rest of the sleeping world – until now. Their mad skills in creative cussing and liberal use of foul language earn them yet another "Best in the World" title.

On the surface, Finns may appear shy, introverted and meek. They don't engage in small talk, and they don't ask idle questions. When they do ask a question, they really want to hear the answer. Which often leads foreigners to conclude that Finns are somewhat childlike in their bluntness and taking things literally. Or that they are all assholes. Neither is actually true. Finns have the highest average IQ in all of Europe, and consistently rank on top, as one of the best educated nation in the world. They most certainly have the smarts, it's just that you may not yet understand the core of the Finnish culture and personality. 97% of Finns younger than 35 years old speak more than one language fluently. Although most Finns speak fluent English, the cultural nuances, like a greeting that sounds like a riddle, and encourages you to look upward for an answer, are sometimes lost on a Finn. For example, if one were to ask them, "What's up?", the likely response could be in all seriousness, "The sky." The question could leave them scratching their heads, wondering why did you ask such a dumb question in the first place. This goes both ways though. Even if you had learned to speak impeccable, grammatically correct, school-taught Finnish, you would completely miss the meaning of some every day Finnish sayings like: "*Sillä Sipuli -* **It's an onion**." (Which by the way translates to "It's a wrap/That's it.") Or if someone were to ask you "*Miksi naamasi on norsunvitulla? -* **Why does your face look like an elephant's cunt?**" You might confuse this as a crude insult, when in fact it was meant to be a compassionate offer of help and an attempt to cheer you up.

To make sure we didn't misrepresent the land of the midnight sun or any of its inhabitants, we consulted with some of the best translators and interpreters working in the field of Finnish – English translations, most of which are native Finns. We made sure that the places, as well as the other parts of the book that required translation, are translated as literally as possible to ensure the accuracy of the content. Our panel of experts have weight in on different parts of the book, making sure that what you will read in the following pages is not only thoroughly entertaining, but also accurate and true. To stay consistent throughout the book, you will find the Finnish word or a saying written in *italics* and its literal English translation in **bold** letters.

This book was designed to guide you through the multiple, hidden, complex layers of Finnish culture, in a way that has not been done before. It will help you look past the seemingly emotionless, quiet exterior of a typical stoic Finn and show you the true nature of Finland, *the* funniest fucking country in the world.

Places

Just consider that Finland has thousands of places that have a cuss word or a sex organ in their name. You read that right – yes – sex organ, and not just the sugarcoated dual meaning versions of these words that would translate to something like Wiener, Beaver or Bush, although those exist too, but as in straight-up Dick, Pussy, Cunt and Cock. They have it all. On the map. And then some.

Many of the surprising place names in Finland are rather tame, such as **Hells Lake** - *Helvetinjärvi*, of which there are 4 in the country. Some are more plentiful, like **Shit Pond** – *Paskalampi*, which number almost 500. Sounds like an awful lot of Shit Ponds, but to put it in perspective, consider that there are approximately 150,000 ponds in Finland, so Shit Ponds only make up about 0.3% of them. There are 2,944 items on the Finnish map that has the word *Paska* – 'Shit' in it, making it overwhelmingly the most popular naughty place name in the country. It's worth mentioning that back when these places had their shitty christenings, the word 'Shit' was not considered much of a profanity. Oh, the good old days.

Some names get more creative and consequently much more entertaining, such as **Fungus Cunt Meadow** – *Kääpävitunaho* or **Big Shit Pines** – *Iso Paskahongikko*.

Few points of interest in Finland

and their literal translations

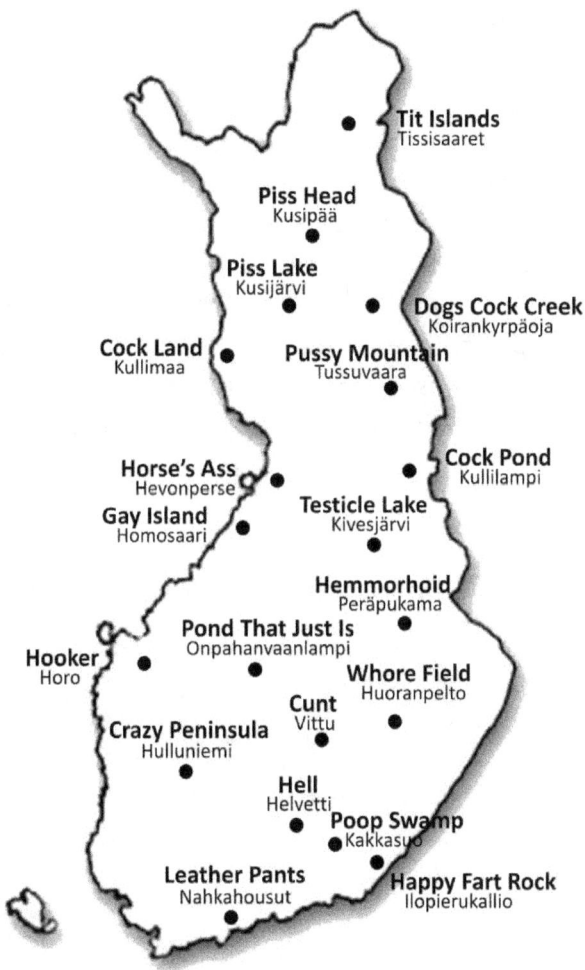

Tit Islands
Tissisaaret

Piss Head
Kusipää

Piss Lake
Kusijärvi

Dogs Cock Creek
Koirankyrpäoja

Cock Land
Kullimaa

Pussy Mountain
Tussuvaara

Horse's Ass
Hevonperse

Cock Pond
Kullilampi

Gay Island
Homosaari

Testicle Lake
Kivesjärvi

Hemmorhoid
Peräpukama

Pond That Just Is
Onpahanvaanlampi

Hooker
Horo

Whore Field
Huoranpelto

Cunt
Vittu

Crazy Peninsula
Hulluniemi

Hell
Helvetti

Poop Swamp
Kakkasuo

Leather Pants
Nahkahousut

Happy Fart Rock
Ilopierukallio

Shitty Places

As we mentioned, almost 500 **Shit Ponds** - *Paskalampi* or *Paskolampi* pepper the landscape of this northern land. In fact, **Shit Pond** is the second most popular name for all of the ponds in Finland, second only to **Black Pond** - *Mustalampi*. These boggy water holes are often too deep to see the bottom of, as the water tends to be murky brown. It is kind of surprising that the most popular pond name in Finland, is not something closer resembling the deep dark hole where the namesake dark matter comes from and where the sun don't shine. Only 8 out of 150,000 ponds are named **Ass Pond** – *Perselampi*. There are 3 rivers in Finland called **Shit River** – *Paskajoki* and *Paskasaari* – **Shit Island** is also found on the map, as is **Shit Mountain** - *Paskatunturi*. The point is, there are plenty of shitty places to visit in Finland if you so choose.

Enjoying Nature

Raija: "Do you want to go hiking this weekend?"

Pirkko: "Sure! How does the Weasel Piss Swamp sound? I hear the native rhododendrons are in full bloom and absolutely stunning."

Raija: "Great! Let's swing by Shit Hill on the way back, I want to see if the bilberries are ripe already."

Some of our absolute favorites in the poop and pee category place names are *Hätäpaskanlähde* aka **Emergency Shit Spring**, **Manure Lake** - *Sonnanjärvi* and **Shat While Running** - *Juostenpaskattu.*

Other shitty places:

- **Shit Crotch** - *Paskahaara*
- **Shit Vacation** - *Paskaloma*
- **The Island Shat by Saara** - *Saaranpaskantamasaari*
- **Rectum River Road** - *Peräsuolijoentie*
- **Hags Ass** - *Ämmänperse*
- **Shit Grease** - *Paskarasva*
- **Big Shit Bog** - *Isopaskaletto*
- **Moose Shit Land** - *Hirvenpaskamaa*
- **Weasel Piss Swamp** - *Kärpänkusisuo*

Oh Saara

Veijo: "Look at the back on her."

Kauko: "Damn. I bet she could shit an island."

Veijo: "I bet you're right! How is your

             wife Saara anyway?"

If you can be like anyone, be like Saara, and have your epic shit memorialized in the most everlasting way.

Origin stories

Finns have named places with vulgar names for as long as there have been places, Finns, or vulgar words. Many of these names date back hundreds of years. It's just not that big of a deal in Finland to live near a place called **Tit Bottom** - *Tissinpohja* or camp at **Cock Forest** - *Kyrpäkorpi*. Surely, they chuckle, but it's all in good humor. Not many find such places all that offensive, although there are a few sticklers that gather a petition every once in a while, trying to change the name of a place, but it is always in vain. The official government stance on the issue is, that naughty place names are part of Finland's cultural heritage, and they are here to stay. When reading a map provides you with endless hours of entertainment, you don't ask questions, you just consider yourself lucky, and thoroughly entertained.

There is a rumor that back in the old days, there were many more creatively named places, up to about 10% of places were said to be naughty, but many of them were rumored to have gotten cleaned out as the officials started drawing maps of the land. *Siitinjärvi* could have been changed to *Siilinjärvi*, changing **Penis Lake** into **Hedgehogs Lake**. *Vittujärvi* may have been changed to *Vattujärvi*, changing the meaning from **Cunt Lake** to **Raspberry Lake**. What a shame. What a shame indeed.

Why name places with such vulgar words? Many of the places are said to have resembled the word they were named after. For example, the shape of the **Penis Peninsula** -

Siitinniemi is likely quite phallic. The trees in **Fungus Cunt Meadow** – *Kääpävitunaho* may have been riddled with polypores that looked eerily similar to wrinkly old beef curtains. **Shit Hill** – *Paskamäki* may have just been a completely useless piece of rocky shit land, riddled with dangerous vipers, or particularly rough terrain that people should avoid. Hence the names also worked as a warning for travelers. Stay away from **Big Shit Bog**- *Isopaskaletto*, no good will come from going there and you might end up getting sucked down in one of its many bog eyes. However, there is also a theory of mapmaking that is quite opposite to the one above. Supposedly, when Finland still suffered under Russian rule, the Russian officials decided to draw out maps of Finland. Russian mapmakers crisscrossed the land asking locals what the names of the villages, lakes, peninsulas, and rivers were. Cheeky Finns told their oppressors names that were actually not accurate. They made them up just to fuck with the Russians. According to this story however, these maps were so well made, that the Finns ended up keeping the maps, and the naughty names on them.

Whatever the origin story of these hilarious places, no one really cares, or gives a fuck, unless it is given as a name for a place. We are just thankful that there is a **Dogs Cock Creek** – *Koirankyrpäoja* and **Hags Fart** - *Ämmänpieru* to enjoy in the middle of the most pristine Finnish nature.

Private Parts

Over time, Finns have named 425 likely bulging landmarks with names that include a form of male genitalia (*Mulkku, Kyrpä, Kulli or Muna*) in its name. For example, there are 3 **Dick Ponds** – *Mulkkulampi* and 9 **Dick Islands** – *Mulkkusaari,* - one of them conveniently located in the middle of **Testicle Lake** – *Kivesjärvi*. Naturally.

These lovable people don't just prefer the male anatomy in terms of naming places. After all, they live in a country that truly believes in gender equality. In all fairness, much of the credit for the country's gender equality belongs to Finland's leading women's rights activist, who turned out to be a real cunt. No really. That was her name. Minna Canth. Pronounced Cunt. Not kidding. Google it. She lived in the 1800's and set Finland on the right path to become the most gender equal country in the world.

Nearly 200 lakes or ponds have the word cunt - *vittu* in them. That's just the lakes and ponds. Now add up all the **Twat Creeks** – *Pillupuro* and **Pussy Rapids** – *Tussukoski*, and the number of places with the words *Vittu, Pillu* and *Tussu*, skyrockets up to 632.

Tit Islands – *Tissisaaret,* **Tit Bottom** – *Tissinpohja* or just plain and simple **Tit** – *Tissi* can also be found on the map, along many other fun and busty places to visit.

Our panels favorite private part place names are as follows, although not in any particular order, we truly love them all equally:

- **Cock Forest** - *Kyrpäkorpi*
- **Penis Peninsula** - *Siitinniemi*
- **Lower Dick** - *Ala-Mulkku*
- **Upper Dick** - *Ylä-Mulkku*
- **Between the Dicks** - *Mulkkujenväli*
- **Ball Wax** - *Pallivaha*
- **Maija's Dick** - *Maijanmulkku* (Yes, Maija is a girl's name in Finland too.)
- **Schlong** - *Lerssi*
- **Pussy Rapids** - *Tussukoski*
- **Whistling Cunt Swamp** - *Viheltävänvitunaapa*
- **Horses Cunt Lake** - *Hevonvittujärvi*
- **Annamari's Crotch** - *Annamarinhaara*
- **Priests Wife's Cunt** - *Ruustinnanpillu*
- **Pussy Tongue Peak** - *Vitunkielipää*
- **Bit by Pussy** - *Pillunpurema* – (Ouch!)
- **Cock Strangling Island** - *Kullinkuristus saari*

I know what you are thinking. What happened to Middle Dick? **Middle Dick** - *Keskimulkku* indeed does exist. It is located in Oulunjärvi. Finland does not disappoint. Ever.

Sometimes vulgar place names are included in the everyday phrases to emphasize a certain meaning. For example, a mother might ask their teenage son, as he is heading out the door in the evening:

Mom: "Where are you going Pekka?"

If Pekka is a true rebel and an avid cusser, as many teenagers are, he might answer something like this:

Pekka: "*Hevonvitunkankaalle mustikkaan.*"

Which roughly translates to:

Pekka: "Picking bilberries at the Horses Cunt Forest."

Now of course, Pekka, a 17-year old tough guy, has no intentions of going out and foraging for berries at that hour, but rather smoke cigarettes and spit on the ground by the local convenience store. What he simply means is:

Pekka: "None of your fucking business."

Mom: "Smell shit Pekka. Dinner is still at 7."

Boozy places

Finns are not exactly known for spitting in a bottle, so to speak. They love their liquor, always have and always will. The booze culture also shows up in the place names, and even surpasses many of the genitalia-related names in volume. With 9 **Moonshine Islands** – *Pontikkasaari,* 14 **Booze Islands** – *Viinasaari* and 18 **Booze Mountains** – *Viinavuori* – It seems that the hard to get to landmarks were often used as secret distilleries during the prohibition. Oh, who are we kidding, Finns have had their secret moonshine factories hidden in the woods, way before prohibition, during it and after it, and perhaps still do. Although hard alcohol is widely distributed in state liquor stores across the country, these luxury goods are still heavily taxed and pricey.

Fun places to add to your boozy bucket list:

- **Booze Gutter** - *Viinaränni*
- **Christmas Booze Hill** - *Joulu-Viinavaara*
- **First Beer Pond** - *Ensimmäinen Kaljalampi*
- **Damnation** - *Hunninko*
- **Death** - *Kuolema*

Hunninko and *Kuolema* of course, are not directly alcohol related places, but it is where you will inevitably end up, if you keep knocking back on grandma's cough medicine one too many times. You have been warned.

Other Improper Places

Creative place names in Finnish are definitely not limited to feces, alcohol and genitalia. Although those are often the most talked about, when funny places in Finland are mentioned. There are many other creatively named locations that deserve their 15 minutes of fame as well. Take **Whore Field** – *Huoranpelto* for example. **Piss Head** – *Kusipää*, **Hooker** – *Horo* and **Fucking Lake** – *Naimajärvi,* they are all there too.

Other geographic areas of interest:

- **Gay Island** - *Homosaari*
- **Coitus** - *Varvi*
- **Hemorrhoid** - *Peräpukama*
- **Baked by Ass** - *Perseenpaistama*
- **Happy Fart Rock** - *Ilopierukallio*

A common theme seems to be the mixing of profanity with nature and landmarks. It is not only fun, but as it turns out, it's also good for marketing. The city of Kuusamo has embraced this perhaps in the most profound way. They now promote day trips to **Butt** - *Pyllykkä*, fishing excursions to **Horses Ass** – *Hevonperse* and **Piss Creek** - *Kusipuro*, hikes to **Dick Mountain** - *Munavaara*, **Pussy Mountain** - *Tussuvaara* and **Fart Hill** - *Pierumäki*. This northern area lives on tourism, and they have figured out a way to get people there. Well played Kuusamo, well played indeed.

Not So Naughty Places

A place can certainly be named creatively without the use of any foul language at all. Not surprisingly, Finns seemed to have mastered this skill as well. According to the National Land Survey of Finland, the following places do exist in the land of thousand lakes. Or should we say, land of hundreds of shit ponds?

Keeping it clean

- **Cat Spankers Alley** - *Kissanpiiskaajankuja*
- **Gangrene** - *Kuolio*
- **Akward** - *Hankala*
- **Boogeyman Line** - *Mörkölinja*
- **Discipline** - *Kuri*
- **Regret** - *Katuma*
- **Crazy Peninsula** - *Hulluniemi*
- **Leather Pants** - *Nahkahousut*
- **Pond That Just Is** - *Onpahanvaanlampi*
- **Valley of the Quiet Men** - *Hiljaisten miesten laakso*

As Finnish men are notoriously quiet and often painfully introverted, pretty much every valley in Finland with men in it, is a Valley of the Quiet Men. Unless it's a Booze Valley, then they talk.

Cat Spankers Alley

Not many oddly named places in Finland spark such curiosity as does the Cat Spankers Alley. We are happy to tell all of you animal lovers, that the name has absolutely nothing to do with spanking a cat. This street is located in Kristiinankaupunki, and was named way back in the days of schooners. Back in those days, a common punishment for unruly or lazy sailors was getting whipped with a nine-stranded whip, called a 'Cat of Nine Tails'. This torture device was popular in the British navy between 1500's – 1800's, to give you an idea of when the street may have been named. Kristiinankaupunki is a harbor town and the term Cat Spanker must have migrated there with the sailors who visited the harbor.

Given this fact, that the street was named hundreds of years ago, it is safe to say that it also had nothing to do with kinky sex, even if the Cat of Nine Tails is still used in those circles to this day. **Cat Spankers Alley** - *Kissanpiiskaajankuja* is located in the old part of Kristiinankaupunki between some very old buildings and measures only 299cm at its narrowest part. It has been deemed to be the 3rd narrowest street in all of Finland. It is a popular tourist attraction, not only because of its creative name, but also due to the bronze metal placement in the 'Narrowest road in the country' competition.

Lazy Names

At some point in time, Finnish land surveyors must have gotten tired of naming places all together or perhaps they were hung over that day and just said fuck it. Either way, they got lazy and came up with some seriously underwhelming spots on the map. These pale in comparison to the earlier mentioned poetic gems such as **Weasel Piss Swamp** and **Fungus Cunt Meadows**, but after careful consideration they do have an aura of quiet amusement just the same.

Short and Sweet

- **Dumb** - *Pöljä*
- **Tight** - *Tiukka*
- **Knee** - *Polvi*
- **Ham** - *Kinkku*
- **Pot** - *Kattila*
- **Hot** - *Kuuma*
- **Fist** - *Koura*
- **Flip** - *Voltti*

It's as if the people in charge of names sat around a campfire, trying feverishly to think of names as the deadline was looming. It's possible they may have been making some hot ham in a pot, done some flips, hurt their knee, and got in a fist fight for calling someone dumb. Think dammit, think!

Sayings and idioms

Given the rather quiet and reserved nature of a typical Finn who carefully considers every word they say, it is all the more unexpected and often downright hilarious, when the few words they choose to say are not the ones fit for the daytime television. Inappropriate idioms may be the Finns way of dealing with the dark and cold winters and to put a little smile on the face of that loved one who may be showing signs of falling into a depression due to the lack of sunlight. Cussing has been said to be therapeutic and decrease stress levels, and no doubt, Finns have perfected this form of therapy like no other nation on earth. Here are some of the nationally treasured idioms that are held near and dear to any true Finns heart.

"If your aunt had a dick, she would be your uncle"

– *Jos tädillä olisi munat, niin se olisi setä.*

This is often used as a way of saying, IF does not count, or stop coming up with excuses. As in:

Olavi: "I would have been on time if it wasn't for the bad weather."

Jorma: "Sure you would have, and if your aunt had a dick, she would be your uncle."

"Messed up like Peterson's pig's pussy hair"

– *Sekaisin kuin Simppasen sian vitun karvat*

This is an old-timey saying that can be used when things are annoyingly out of order or totally messed up.

 "Who the hell made this log pile? It's as messed up as Peterson's pig's pussy hair!"

Things can get a little heated if your log pile for the winter does not look ruler precise.

Editor's note: We took artistic liberty in changing the name Simppanen to Peterson to make it rhyme better in English.

"Rolls around like a lingonberry in the pussy."

– *Pyörii kuin puolukka pillussa.*

This saying refers to something that is having difficulty staying still, and trying to keep this item stationery is getting frustrating. For example:

"I am trying to cut my kids hair, but he is rolling around like a lingonberry in the pussy! Damn that kid. Now his hair is messed up like Peterson's pig's pussy hair."

Lingonberries ending up in peoples' baby makers have a longstanding history in Finland. It is not clear if this saying originated from the Finnish National Epic *Kalevala* or not, but it's definitely possible. Within those ancient poems and songs that have been passed on for hundreds of years, from generation to generation, lurks a story about a virgin being impregnated by a single lingonberry. The child born from this immaculate conception grew up to be a hero and a stud, who beat the old reining hero *Väinämöinen*. Not to mention, he also started talking in full sentences at two weeks of age. Since there was no father in the picture, and the mother was obviously a dirty, dirty whore in eyes of everyone, the child was not allowed to be named. In fact, Väinämöinen ordered the child to be killed, perhaps knowing that if he were allowed to stay alive, it would be the end of Väinämöinen one day. However, after the two-week old baby heard of these plans, he started talking shit to the Ol' Väinämöinen, saying "Hey, you old git! You caused your young bride to drown herself! Because you were so old and nasty, she would rather die than be forced to marry you. You caused her death, so if I am supposed to be killed, so are you." – Väinämöinen had to agree, bastard had a point. So Väinämöinen backed off, named the kid *Karjalan Kuningas* - the King of Karelia and left without a further ado. The end. Moral of the story: Don't mess around with lingonberries, or you might end up being a single mother of some weird shit talking infant. Better safe than sorry girls.

Sayings about looks

- **Face like an elephant's cunt** - *Naama norsunvitulla.* This face is an unhappy or a cranky one. A person displaying this expression could use a hug.

- **Dick on forehead** - *Kyrpä otsassa.* Person with a dick on their forehead is unhappy or pissed off. As we suppose one would be, should a glorious pizzle suddenly sprout out of your brow making you into some kind of a perverted dick headed unicorn.

- **Swallowed a dick** – *Kyrvän niellyt.* This means a person in question is unhappy or angry.

At work

Jorma: "Hey Olavi, why does Reiska look like he swallowed a dick?"

Olavi: "I think his wife told him he can't go to the party tonight."

Jorma: "Oh that sucks, I would have a dick on my forehead too if Raija pulled that shit."

- **Face like a raptor's ass** - *Naama kuin petolinnun perse.* This face is hideously ugly.

- **Eyes like on a shitting pigs** – *Silmät kuin sittuvalla sialla.* These eyes are squinting and on the small side. Like if you just sucked on a lemon.

- **Pig ugly** – *Sika ruma.* – Very ugly. You can also use the word *Sika* – **Pig** in front of anything to emphasize the meaning, as in, **Pig fancy** – *sika hieno* is fancier than just plain fancy, **Pig large** – *sika iso* is very large. You get the 'piggly' picture. Put pig in front of any adjective and it means more.

At the bar

Raija: "He's kind of hot don't you think?"

Pirkko: "Are you kidding me? His face looks like a raptor's ass. Did you forget your glasses again?!"

Raija: "Spring of cunts and a returning winter of cocks! I thought I was wearing them."

(Pulls glasses out of purse and puts them on)

Raija: "Oh shit, you're right! Nice ass though."

Other naughty phrases and idioms

- **Rains like from Ester's ass** - *Sataa kuin Esterin perseestä.* – A very hard rain or a downpour. You can keep your cats and dogs, Ester's ass is where it's at for the Finns. You can also say:

- **Rains like shaft** – *Sataa kuin aisaa.* We are not sure how this came to be, but as there is only one kind of shaft we can think of, that routinely expels liquid, we can only guess about the origin of this one. It also means that it is raining heavily.

- **Fingers are like a stack of dicks** - *Sormet ovat kuin nippu mulkkuja.* These fingers are fat, stiff and often useless for tasks requiring dexterity.

- **Twisted like a hog's cock** – *Kiero kuin karjun kyrpä.* This can be used to describe an item that is bent or twisted. It can also be used to describe a person who is untrustworthy and crooked. A real wicked bastard.

- **Comma fucker** - *Pilkun nussija.* A person that is particularly anal or pedantic.

- **Ladybug fucker** – *Leppäkertun nussija,* means the same exact thing as 'comma fucker' but sounds more whimsical. Ladybugs have dots, or commas if you will, and it would take a rather meticulous and detail orientated person to get the job done

- **Like a cock of a crazy in the ass of a mindless** - *Kuin hullun kulli mielettömän perseessä*. This is used to describe something that is limp or useless, definitely not turgid, stiff or useful in any way. This can also be used to describe something that moves around uncontrollably. Flopping around without purpose as one can imagine a crazy man's flaccid penis would be, trying to pound the ass of a person who is obviously out of their mind. No sane person would ever let someone sodomize them with a completely limp dick. A great saying that has been used for several generations.

- **Like a mosquito's fart in the Sahara desert** – *Kuin hyttysen pieru Saharassa*. This is used to describe something insignificant. As such, a mosquito's fart in the Sahara doesn't matter much, if at all. It can also be used as a way of describing something that has completely vanished without a trace: 'Disappeared like a mosquito's fart in the Sahara desert'.

- **Going hunting in the dick forest** - *Lähteä munametsälle*. This one is reserved for women and gay men, and means you are going out for the night, with the intentions of finding a man.

- **Leaving something like a dog leaves its shit** - *Jättää kuin koira paskansa.* This means that things are left lying around in the wrong place, and it creates a mess. This is a good one for the mothers who must constantly remind their children to pick up their coats and put away their shoes which were carelessly left in the middle of the floor. Like a dog would leave its shit, never worrying about who has to pick it up.

- **Sunset colors, good colors, sunrise colors, shit colors** - *Iltarusko hyvä rusko, aamurusko päivän paska.* - This is practically the same thing as "Red sky at night, sailors delight. Red sky in morning, sailors warning" but when in Rome, we mean in Finland, the word shit is added for extra entertainment and authenticity.

- **Let's go cows, the bull has a boner** - *Let's go lehmät, sonnilla seisoo.* This is used among the ladies, trying to heard the whole group of them into some sort of activity. Likely drinking, or to go hunting in the dick forest, or both.

- **Shitty end for the greedy** – *Ahneella on paskainen loppu.* – Don't be greedy, it will never end well.

- **Pissed while running** – *Juosten kustu*. This can be used to describe a shoddy job. It is evident that whoever completed this task was extremely careless, lazy, in a hurry or all of the above. It looks like the marks of urination made on the ground while running.

- **Like a bear shot in the ass** - *On kuin perseeseen ammuttu karhu.* This description is reserved for a person who is angry, or extremely agitated, possibly both. Better leave them alone and back away slowly without making any eye contact.

- **Just in case, like the nun's nipples** – *Varmuuden vuoksi, niin kuin nunnan nännit.* You could just as well say, 'just in case', but it's always fun to throw some nips into the game. This pearl of a sentence can also be used to describe something quite unnecessary, such as 'not needed like a nun's nipples'.

- **Runny nose is healed by fucking** - *Nuha lähtee nussimalla.* Oldie but goody, also quite self-explanatory. Try it sometime. If it has worked for Finns for hundreds of years, it will work for you too. And if not, at least you got laid.

- **Fits like a fist in the eye** - *Sopii kuin nyrkki silmään.* This is used, when something fits in place particularly well, flawlessly even. An American would say, "fits like a glove", but where's the fun in that?

- **Fits like a cobbler's finger in a pig's ass** - *Sopii kuin suutarin sormi sian perseeseen.* Same as above. Something fits in place very nicely indeed. Nowadays these hardworking, footwear fixing artisans have almost completely given up the practice of poking their fingers up the asses of animals.

- **Go on one's thighs** – *Mennä reisille.* Essentially this means 'to fail'. Something went wrong and you did not succeed in whatever it was you were trying to do. This saying is widely used and is in reference to a premature ejaculation that ended up on a woman's thighs, instead of inside her lady-garden where it was intended.

- **Only option, is to put them back, and fuck again** - *Ei voi kuin laittaa takaisin ja nussia uudestaan.* An old-timey morsel of gold, that is used to describe a person that is bad, hopeless or useless. They are such a failure, that the only way to fix them is to put them back where they came from, fuck again and make another child with the hopes that the next one will turn out better.

- **Shit flies like a flock of sparrows** – *Paska lentää kuin varpusparvi.* – You ate something that did not agree with your old gullet, or you caught a bug. Either way you are now suffering from explosive diarrhea. A.K.A. you have the shits of the worst uncontrollable kind.

- **Thin as a wheezy grass fucked by the prairie wind** – *Laiha kuin arotuulen nussima vinkuheinä.* This person is extremely thin, malnourished and sickly.

- **Fucked by frost** – *Hallan panema.* Your spring garden or wheat field is 'fucked by frost' when mother nature decides, in mid-June, that it's time for some below freezing temps for a few nights.

- **Rolls around like a fart in the leather pants** – *Pyörii kuin pieru nahkahousuissa.* – Something is stuck or rolling around without a purpose and without an easy exit. Just like a cloud of methane would, in tight pants made of animal hide.

- **Grouse Shit** – *Teeren Paska.* – This is just another name for freckles. Often used in a way: 'They had grouse shit on their nose.' i.e. 'The fellow had freckles.'

- **Turns into thousand pussy shingles** - *Menee tuhannen pillunpäreiksi.* This is an interesting one for sure. It means that something is thoroughly destroyed and beyond repair. As in:

Pekka: "I dropped the crystal vase and it turned into thousand pussy shingles. Mom is going to kill me when she finds out. It was their wedding present."

Mikko: "Oh man, you are in real piss. Pirkko will ground your ass for at least a month!"

It is worth mentioning, that since the word shingles has a few different definitions, this one means the thin slabs of wood that are used to cover the roof of a house. As wooden shingles are almost never found in vaginas, this doesn't appear to make much sense. However, back in the old days, wooden shingles were used as a single use seat cover for the sauna, where you would sit your bare bottom onto the 'pussy shingle' – *pillunpäre*, to keep the sauna bench clean. It is unclear to us, how exactly the 'pussy shingle' was so thoroughly destroyed, and how this saying came to be, but regardless, it still ranks high on our all-time favorites list.

- **This won't result in a child or a shit** – *Tästä ei tule lasta eikä paskaa.* This means you are failing. Or rather when you are in the middle of a task and it is becoming evident that you are headed toward failure. The roots of this saying are in child birth and the fact that one often soils themselves when pushing a watermelon size chunk of a human being out of their baby cannon. The ultimate failure in this situation indeed would be if you ended up with neither a child nor shit.

Deathly sayings

Death comes to us all. It is inevitable and often unpleasant for everyone involved. But how we choose to talk about it is up to us and could make all the difference in the grieving process. Here are some examples of how Finns do it.

- **Throw a spoon in the corner** – *Heittää lusikan nurkkaan.* – If one 'threw a spoon in the corner' – they are definitely all the way dead.

- **Throw the cranks** – *Heittää veivit.* "Crank" here translates to the kind of crank they used to start a car or other simple machinery with. You don't want to 'throw your cranks' as it means that you have passed away.

- **Kick emptiness/miss kick** – *Potkaista tyhjää.* Just like the two previous examples, this means that one is perished. If grandpa kicked emptiness, it is high time to call the coroner.

- **Take someone behind the sauna** – *Viedä saunan taakse.* This one is a bit on the darker side, and means to kill someone, or beat the shit out of them. Either way if someone takes you behind the sauna, you may end up dead. In the old days, this out-of-sight place was often used to slaughter animals. Should someone invite you to join them behind the sauna, just say no. The best-case scenario is that you will end up as an accomplice. Worst case, you throw the cranks.

Measurements and time

Finns are known for being punctual and accurate. In addition to actual time and distance telling, they have developed some rather creative ways to tell the passage of time as well as various forms of measurements.

- **Slip of a dick** - *Kullin luikaus.* This means 'fast', 'just a sec' or 'it won't take long'.

Car pooling

Jorma: "Can you stop by the liquor store, since we are driving right past it?"

Olavi: "No. We are running late as it is."

Jorma: "Oh come on, it won't take but a slip of a dick, I already know what I'm getting."

Olavi: "Fine. But I will tell them it's your fault we didn't make it there on time."

Jorma: "Relax Olavi. It's a party, no one cares if we are on time anyway."

If you have ever lived in Finland, you know that Jorma here is dead wrong, and that everyone will care if you are on time, and especially if you aren't. Being even a little bit late, is considered rude by most Finns and is definitely frowned upon.

- **Five till a pussy hair** – *Viittä vaille vitun karvaa*. This is usually only used when someone asks you what time it is, or what time something is due to begin and you A) Don't know, or don't feel like telling them B) Don't care what time it is C) You feel like it's none of their business. Similar to American saying "Half past a monkey's ass, quarter to his balls."

About damn time

Mikko: "Hey Pekka, what time is it?"

Pekka: "Five till a pussy hair. How about you finally
            get your own fucking watch so you don't have
            to always ask?"

Mikko: "You are such a cunt head sometimes."

Pekka: "Go to cunt."

Mikko: "You go to cunt."

- **Dicks measure** – *Mulkun mitta*. This means a length
  of a penis, which of course can vary greatly.
  According to the internet, an average flaccid,
  pendulous human penis is 9.16 cm or 3.61" in length.
  Whereas an average erect penis is 13.12 cm or 5.16".
  As the 'Dicks measure' does not specify whether the
  penis in question is parade ready or completely limp,
  we can only assume 'Dicks measure' means
  anywhere between 3 and 6 inches. We are however,
  fairly sure the dick in question is that of a human, and
  not for example, that of an elephant, which of course
  would throw off the measurement greatly.

At the office parking lot

Jorma: "Hey Olavi, you might want to go move your car. Your tire is outside the line by about a dicks measure on passenger side."

Olavi: "Thanks Jorma. Will do, I'd hate to get keyed or worse. I was running late this morning, hence the shitty park job."

- **Reindeer pissing** - *Poron kusema*. There are about 200,000 reindeer in Finland, and although most of them roam free, they are also used for transportation in the rough northern terrain. 'Reindeer pissing' is the distance a reindeer can go without eliminating its bladder. The actual distance can vary, but it will not exceed 7.5 kilometers or 4.6 miles. Reindeer are incapable of peeing while running, and if not allowed to pee regularly, Rudolph may end up having a seizure. Piss breaks for reindeer are super important. Who knew? So next time when you are riding around in a reindeer sleigh, be a good sport and make sure to let the animal urinate at least every 7.5 km.

Girls night in

Raija: "Hey Pirkko, you want to come over? I would love to catch up over a sauna and some drinks."

Pirkko: "I don't know Raija. I was out last night and you are like three reindeer pissings away. That seems so far away right now."

Raija: "Whatever, I can come pick you up and you can stay the night. It will be fun."

Pirkko: "In that case! Let me just make sure there's some pizza in the freezer for Pekka. Should I bring beer?"

Raija: "No need, I have a whole case of cranberry Lonkero that I brought home from Estonia."

Pirkko: "Great! I'll be ready in an hour."

Natural world

Finns love their nature and take protecting the beautiful landscape very seriously. They are world leaders in coexisting with the nature that surrounds them. There are however, a few exceptions in Finnish nature, that have not won the hearts of the people.

- **Shit Jay** – *Paskanärhi*. *Närhi*, or Jay, is a dirty scavenger bird, much like the crow or magpie. They dig through the garbage for treats, and are generally a nuisance. You could just say 'Jay', but it is not uncommon to hear them called 'Shit Jay', regardless of the fact that the Finnish Jay is actually a very pretty bird.

- **Shit Rowan** – *Paskapihlaja*. Despite its beautiful clusters of red berries, this tree is not related to the Rowan tree - *Pihlaja*. Rowan is considered a sacred tree in Finland and is often the first tree one plants in their back yard upon purchasing a home. 'Shit rowan' is the native Red Elderberry, and its real Finnish name is *Terttuselja*. Its nick name is so commonplace though that only the most dedicated plant enthusiasts would be able to tell you its official name. For everyone else, it is simply 'Shit Rowan'.

Clean yet funny sayings

- **Matti in your wallet** – *Matti kukkarossa.* – This means your wallet is empty. Matti is a common male name in Finland and this could just as well be Antti or Pekka, but for some unknown reason Matti was chosen to be the symbol of all things broke and penniless.

- **Heck's sixteen** – *Hemmetin kuustoista.* – This expresses frustration but in a way that can be said in front of a kindergartener, similar in usage to 'Gosh Darned'.

- **Run with your head as a third leg** – *Juosta pää kolmantena jalkana.* – Rushing around, moving fast in a panicked way, not necessarily accomplishing a lot, but looking super busy nevertheless.

- **Throw some lip** – *Heittää huulta.* – If you are throwing some lip, you are talking in a joking manner.

- **Mouth on brass** – *Suu messingillä.* – If one has their mouth on brass, it does not mean they have golden teeth or other unsightly dental bling. It simply means they are smiling.

- **We are not riding a rabbit** – *Ei tässä jäniksen selässä olla.* – This means 'We are not in that much of a hurry' or 'We have plenty of time, you can slow down a little'.

- **Through a gray rock** – *Läpi harmaan kiven.* – This means you will not give up, ever, no matter what. It perfectly expresses the spirit of "Finnish Sisu" or perseverance, meaning that you will not give up, but will go through a gray rock if need be. Healthy, or sometimes not so healthy stubbornness is an essential building block of a Finn. They don't like asking for help and will bang their head against a wall, so-to-speak, until the job is done.

- **Your own cow is in the ditch** – *Oma lehmä ojassa.* – This means you have a stake of your own in something. Very similar to the English version of 'to have some skin in the game'.

- **Fell apart like Jokinen's packed lunch** – *Levisi kuin Jokisen eväät.* – If something falls thoroughly apart, it has the same destiny as Jokinen's packed snacks. Side note: Jokinen is a common last name in Finland, similar in popularity to Johnson in the U.S.

- **Go into the pipe** – *Mennä putkeen.* – This means you have succeeded in a task. If your presentation went into the pipe, it went great! Congrats, you did it!

- **Something goes over the dandruff** – *Menee yli hilseen.* – Very similar to 'Goes over one's head' as in something was not understood, or is difficult to comprehend. We don't believe that the ratio of folks suffering from dandruff or an itchy scalp in Finland is any higher than the rest of the world. The saying has likely been developed purely for the purpose of whimsy.

- **Out like a snowman** – *Pihalla kuin lumiukko.* – This can be used in a similar way as the phrase above. It is typically used when you don't understand something or are having a hard time following a conversation. When you just don't get it, you are out like a snowman.

- **Looking for it with the cats and dogs** – *Etsitään kissojen ja koirien kanssa.* – You have looked and looked for something and have exhausted all means of recovering whatever it is you have lost. You have looked for it with the cats and dogs.

- **It's an onion** – *Sillä sipuli.* – This means 'that's it', 'all done' or 'that's a wrap'. Let's think about the origin of this one for a moment. Actually, let's not, we have no fucking idea. It makes absolutely no sense, and it's an onion.

- **It's an onion, like a big boy's diarrhea** – *Sillä sipuli kuin ison pojan ripuli.* – This means the same exact thing as the one above, only you are feeling a bit more talkative and whimsical than usual. This seems to make even less sense, but we believe this came to be because 'onion – *sipuli*' and 'diarrhea – *ripuli*' rhyme. Pure poetry if you ask us.

- **Cool like a tub of sour yogurt** – *Viileä kuin viilipytty.* This means you are unfazed and calm. No matter what goes on around you, you manage to keep your cool. It can also describe a very calm or stoic personality.

- **Now took a barley bread** – *Nyt otti ohraleipä.* – You have encountered a problem that you are not sure how to solve. Basically, it means 'I have no idea how to do this.' Grammatically this sentence structure makes no sense in Finland either, although you might find a sentence that is build this way in some very old poetry.

- **Be covered in sap** – *Olla pihkassa.* – If you are covered in sap, that means you have a crush on someone.

- **Ten points and a parrot button** – *Kymmenen pistettä ja papukaijamerkki.* – You completed a task beyond anyone's expectations. Not sure why you got a parrot button, but you did, and somehow it matters.

- **Left the mitten** – *Lähteä lapasesta.* – This means basically the same as American saying 'Got out of hand'. For example, you decide to start a new hobby, such as knitting, but instead of knitting responsibly, you end up turning into a yarn hoarder and fill your entire home with colorful skeins of beautiful yarns spun from the wool of all sorts of furry animals. Your excessive yarn buying definitely left the mitten, instead of producing one.

- **The moped ran away from your hands** – *Lähtee mopo käsistä.* – This is basically the same exact thing as leaving the mitten, but might resonate better with the male population of Finland. Most of them, at some point, have owned a moped, yet not many of them might not give much thought to mittens.

- **Grouse Game** – *Teeren Peli.* – If you are 'Grouse Gaming', you are flirting with someone.

45

- **Wing on the ground** – *Siipi maassa.* – A person with a 'wing on the ground' is sad. Give them a hug or bring them a Latte, they will appreciate it.

- **Bubble on your forehead** – *Kupla otsassa* – This means you really have to pee. As in the urine is bubbling up all the way up to your forehead.

I'm drunk, you're drunk, we're all drunk

In Finland, it is not enough to say that one is under the influence of alcohol. There are several stages of drunkenness, that need described in order to communicate in an effective way, and surprisingly none of them are dirty. Seems that Finns go rather easy on their drunks. How drunk someone is exactly, is determined as follows:

- **In a little pretty** – *Pienessä sievässä.* – Person who is 'in a little pretty' is merely tipsy, they have only had a couple of drinks and are still completely coherent and fun to be around.

- **In a taste** – *Olla maistissa.* – You can definitely tell that this person has had a taste of alcohol. They are little more than tipsy, but still climbing up to the 'life of a party' stage of drunkenness. Fun times, and if they pace themselves, this person might very well end up with some fond memories of this night.

- **Around their heads** – *Ympäri päissään.* – If one is 'around their heads', it means he or she is very drunk, they have officially passed the delightfully tipsy stage.

- **Drunk as a cuckoo** – *Kännissä kuin käki.* – This means one is completely wasted. Getting to the state of drunkenness when one is obnoxious, annoying and likely to embarrass themselves and others.

- **Snot drunk** – *Räkäkännissä.* – One is intoxicated enough that they will not notice that the giant snot they hacked up ten minutes ago is stuck to their cheek. For embarrassment purposes, this is usually the most entertaining stage to videotape.

- **In a dead-end tunnel** – *Umpitunnelissa.* – This means one is thoroughly shit faced. Unable to talk coherently, close to passing out. Person is not seeing a lot of light at the end of that tunnel and is getting sleepy.

- **In a dead end drunk** – *Umpihumalassa.* – This is a variation of the above, and means the exact same thing.

- **Hot dogs on eyes** – *Nakit silmillä.* – If you have 'hot dogs on your eyes', you are incredibly drunk, in fact you are very close to passing out. Possible stage 1 alcohol poisoning in process. Not good.

- **Games stopped** – *Pelit seis.* – Your night is officially over. You have passed out and possibly soiled yourself. You may have had fun, but you wouldn't know it, as you can't remember anything from the last several hours. Not surprising, this person sometimes wakes up in the ER as their stomach is being pumped.

Very Finnish Concepts

Kalsarikännit – Underpants Drunk

Finns have invented a wonderful word to describe 'Getting Drunk in your home in your underpants' – or as they would put it *Kalsarikännit*. *Kalsari* quite literally means **underpants** and *Kännit* translates to **drunk**. As a concept, *Kalsarikännit* is not a new one by any measure, but the word to describe it, has only just recently gained in popularity. As a single beer or cider will set you back about 7-12 euros, drinking in Finnish bars can get very expensive. Getting drunk in your home is not only a cost-effective way to relax, but it also cuts back on drunk driving incidents and embarrassing scenes to sort out and apologize for later, as long as you stay out of social media that it. There is no need to fuss over getting all prettied up, or even dressed for that matter! *Kalsarikännit* has become a socially acceptable phenomenon, and the benefits of such homebound drunkenness can't be denied.

Kalsarikännit is Finland's version of Danish Hygge. It is the Finns way to relax and forget about the stresses and expectations of everyday life for a while. Zero out one's brain if you will. All that's needed for *Kalsarikännit* is a comfortable place, such as your home, a friend's home, a hotel room, etc., an adequate amount of alcohol, some snacks and a device of some sort to give you something relaxing to do while you enjoy your evening. Device does not have to be an electronic one, it could be something much more old school, such as a record player, a book, or even a puzzle, although in today's world it is common to spend one's evening with a smart phone, TV or a tablet. This may sound to some, like a saddest way to spend an evening, but it is actually anything but. *Kalsarikännit* can be enjoyed by yourself, or with a close friend. The purpose of *Kalsarikännit* is not to get hot dogs on your eyes and pass out, but rather enjoy a few drinks and forget about your worries in an atmosphere that is as cozy and carefree as being wrapped in a warm blanket.

Sometimes *Kalsarikännit* can lead to a sudden urge to go out and join civilization, and that is OK! There are no strict rules here, and if you decide after a while that a trip to your local pub is in order, go for it!

Happy Hour

Jorma:	"Hey Olavi, are you coming over to the pub after work? It is Friday after all."
Olavi:	"No, I don't think so, I will probably pull an all night kalsarikännit, it's been a shitty week and I feel like getting drunk in my skivvies while listening to some of my favorite tunes."
Jorma:	"Fair enough Ollie, see you Monday."

Sauna

People of Finland have been enjoying the soul soothing effects of the sauna for hundreds, if not thousands of years. In the old days, sauna had many purposes besides bathing. It was the place where women gave birth, sick were treated and the dead were washed and prepared for their final journey. Sauna has always been a holy place to Finns, and even today, it is still treated as a place of quiet meditative mindfulness. There are over 3 million saunas in Finland for a population of roughly 5 million. A typical Finn goes to the sauna 1-2 times a week, usually on Wednesday and Saturday evening. A sauna can be inside your apartment, out in your backyard, by a lake at the summer cottage, or even in a gondola going up and down a mountain. If there's a place with enough room to fit a sauna, a Finn will find it.

Finnish sauna is always enjoyed in the nude, unless it is a coed sauna with people you are not familiar with. Public saunas are separated by gender so you will only come across the body parts you were born with. Sauna is often enjoyed with close friends and co-workers as well as family members. By the time a typical Finn is of that certain age when they start getting interested in an intimate relationship, they have already seen hundreds of naked bodies from various genders, in non-sexual bathing situations. They have seen countless knockers, fur-burgers and peckers in a variety of shapes, sizes and curvatures. They know that 'normal' can look very different depending on the person. A Finns first look at a naked body is never from a nudie mag, and this could at least partly explain the "body positive" way Finns look at themselves and others. To most Finns, the body does not define the person, but rather, their personality does. In part, body positivity is also reinforced in the media, where catalog models, tv actors and actresses, and other public figures are quite normal looking people, just like the rest of them, with varied body types and unique trades.

To a first timer, the Finnish sauna might be a strange experience. Even though saunas have been built around the world in various hotels and health clubs, the real Finnish experience is very different from the foreign spas. As previously mentioned, the Finnish sauna is enjoyed in your birthday suit. It is often hotter than its foreign counter parts, usually about 80-100 Celsius or 176 – 212 Fahrenheit, and the water that is thrown on the *Kiuas* (sauna stove) rocks will make it even hotter as the hot steam fills the small room. Many Finns prefer a log heated stove over the electric one, saying it will give out a softer sauna experience. As the heat of the sauna descends on a person, breathing can get difficult. Take shallow breaths, and move to a lower level if you find it too hot on top. Sauna is always followed by bathing or showering, making you squeaky clean.

Traditionally, *Vihta* is part of a special sauna experience where a bunch of silver birch branches are tied together to make a bouquet-like item. *Vihta*, or as some call it *Vasta*, is used to gently slap each other while in the sauna. It invigorates one's blood circulation and leaves behind a wonderful aroma of birch leaves which also act as aroma therapy. For obvious reasons *Vihta* is typically used in the summer months and on special occasions such as Mid-Summer fest - *Juhannus*, although some *Vihta* enthusiasts like to make them in bulk during the summer and either hang them up to dry or freeze them for later. Nowadays many grocery stores also carry them in their frozen section.

Sauna is often accompanied not only by a bouquet of spanking birch, but also a cooling off period. This can be accomplished by jumping in a lake, rolling in the snow, or just sitting outside or in a separate room outside of the sauna. The idea is to go in, get hot, get out and cool off and then repeat this for a few times. As hydration is important when sweating profusely with your fellow naked Finns, a beer, water, or soda often finds its way to the hands of the bathers. The type of the drink is not important, as long as it's cold and refreshing.

In a nutshell, sauna means you go sweat next to your naked friends, sit on a wooden bench, in a dimly lit room, while spanking each other with some leafy sticks, roll naked in the snow and drink some beers, all the while never forgetting the golden rule of the sauna: Never fart in the sauna, under any circumstances, except if you don't want to be invited back, ever again.

Sisu

Sisu is a Finnish concept that has no directly translatable equivalent in any other language that we know of. People describe *Sisu* as a stoic determination, tenacity of purpose, grit, bravery, resilience, and hardiness. According to Finns themselves, it perfectly expresses their national character. It has also been described as a special strength and the persistence to continue, and overcome, in the moment of adversity. Almost a magical quality. A combination of stamina, perseverance, courage, and blind determination held in reserve for hard times.

Finnish *Sisu* became known worldwide during WWII when Russia attacked Finland under the false assumption that conquering the small country would take about two weeks. Three and a half months later, Russia had lost a quarter million men, with an additional 400,000+ missing, another quarter million wounded and over 5,000 captured. Not to mention over 2,000 tanks that were destroyed or confiscated by the Finnish army. There are many factors that went into the outcome of the famous Winter War, but one of them, most definitely, was the Finnish *Sisu*, where each soldier carried with them a stubbornness and a refusal to give up, no matter how dire the situation may have been. No one was predicting this Lilliputian nation to be able to fend for themselves against the Red Army, yet it happened, and Finland was able to keep their independence when many other nations fell into the long and painful Russian occupation.

For generations, most Finns lived a quiet rural existence, where the nearest neighbors may have been many miles away. The only option really, was to get things done by yourself and not rely on the help of others. In an arctic climate, just surviving daily life required a healthy amount of *Sisu*, and often still does. To this day, most Finnish children walk, bike, or kick-sled their way to school every day, even on the coldest of the winter days. Schools have a mandatory 15-minute recess every hour, during which, the children will go outside to play year around. If the temperatures reach lower than negative 20C (-4F) recess will be held indoors.

In the animal world, *Sisu* is probably best displayed by the ever-persevering Honey Badger. Although this animal is not native to Finland, it might as well be. Just like the toe-headed Finns, honey badgers are total and utter bad asses. Honey badger will go through a gray rock if needed, it will fight to the death against a much bigger foe, and often, end up a winner just through its sheer stubborn craziness. Much like an average Finn, the honey badger doesn't give a shit, and that my friend, is an essential part of not only *Sisu*, but also being a Finn.

Finnish insults or Finnsults

Overall, Finns are kind and non-argumentative folk. Most of them avoid confrontation at all cost in their daily lives. In fact, they are experts at avoiding other people all together and defending their own personal space. This is a key element to peaceful coexistence in small spaces, where many urban dwelling Finns reside. Most of them will peek through their door before entering the communal staircase or any other shared space of the apartment block, just to make sure no one else is out there. Should there be another human being walking around, a Finn will likely wait patiently until the neighbor is out of sight, before entering the area. To many Finns, it is a beautiful thing, if you have shared a wall with someone for 20 years and have never once seen each other face-to-face. This does not happen by accident, but by meticulous planning and expert skills in avoidance. When you rarely see each other, there is very little reason for insults.

Any causes of irritation between the inhabitants living in the same apartment block, are typically addressed through passive aggressive notes left anonymously on the cork board next to the front door of the apartment complex for all to see, thus giving the misbehaving party a chance to get their shit together without confrontation. These notes could address anything from showering after 10pm, listening to loud music or parking your bicycle in a rude manner blocking easy access to other bikes in the communal bicycle shed.

Finns are much more likely to insult each other in closer circles as opposed to flipping birds to complete strangers. Playful banter often takes place between friends after a few drinks, someone gets called a cunt head, while someone else is encouraged to smell shit. These exchanges are almost always forgotten and forgiven the next day. It was just beer-talk anyway, no need to drag it on. Insults can also be incredibly helpful, even to a kind-hearted Finn, when used as a tool to effectively communicate with family members, such as ungrateful and often lazy kids.

The most tried and true insults in Finland are often very olfactory centered. In the midst of a heated argument a Finn will either tell you to smell something foul, or to go away to some unpleasant destination. The English word 'fuck' directly translated - *nussia*, is never used as an insult in Finland, but merely to describe the act of intercourse. In fact, if one would say 'Fuck off' in Finnish – *Nussi pois*, it could be understood to mean "Sure, go ahead and fuck." - That could go south very quickly. No pun intended. Or maybe it was, guess you'll never know for sure.

Here are some of the most common things a person could expect to hear if they should ever anger a Finn.

Smelly Insults, aka 'fuck you'

- **Smell a cunt** - *Haista vittu.* This is the mother of all Finnish insults, equivalent to 'Fuck You'. If someone says this to you, you are probably no longer friends and if you desire to continue the friendship, some serious apologizing may be in order. Don't confuse this as an invitation to sniff anyone's crotch.

- **Smell shit** - *Haista paska.* Similar to *Haista Vittu*, but has lost approximately 30% of its strength. Still a good little insult though, and not a nice thing to say or have said to you. Use sparingly.

- **Smell a flute** - *Haista huilu.* This is just a very nice way to say 'fuck you'. It is mild, but since you are still encouraged to smell something, even if it is just a spit-filled stinky fife, it is still a valid insult.

- **Smell a flower** - *Haista kukkanen.* The mildest of all smelly insults, could even be said to a child, but still a sure sign you are definitely not in agreement. Not to be confused with an invitation to ones fully blooming balcony garden.

Go away Insults, aka 'fuck off'

- **Go to cunt** - *Painu vittuun.* This is the worst insult in the Finnish 'fuck off' family. You have reached a point where fists might soon start flying and fitting neatly into eyes. Similar to 'Get out of my fucking face'. Although the word *Painu* does not directly translate to the word 'go', but rather 'press into' it is used here in a way that means go. Definitely not to be confused with an invitation to press yourself into someone's beaver.

- **Ski to cunt** - *Suksi vittuun.* Same as above, only on skis. Pretty harsh thing to say overall, but if you are past the point of giving a damn, this is a good one to have in your repertoire since it shows off your inventive nature and your love for winter sports.

- **Go to hell** - *Painu helvettiin.* Medium strength go away insult, still potent enough to mean business.

- **Go to goblin** - *Painu hiiteen.* This is the mildest insult in this category. *Hiisi* means many things, for example 'underworld' – 'forest goblin'- (*metsähiisi*) – 'water goblin'- (*vesihiisi*). It can also be translated as 'an unpleasant faraway place'. Take your pick. It still means fuck off, only in one of the nicest ways possible.

Head related insults

As in many cultures, a great many insults include saying something negative about your head. These are all similar in meaning to 'idiot', 'moron' etc. Only the severity and tone of them changes slightly. Here are the Finnish versions of the head related insults, from top to bottom, most severe on top.

- **Cunt head** – *Vittupää*. This has the most oomph compared to all of the other unflattering heads you may be called. *Vittupää* is a person that might not only be utterly stupid, but could also have a hint of evil to them. Indeed, an undesirable person you do not want to associate with, a real fucking reprobate.

- **Shit head** – *Paskapää*. Just a really shitty person to be around, with low morals and shit for brains.

- **Dick head** – *Munapää*. Kind of universal, but just in case you are not familiar with the phrase, this is a person who makes bad decisions and is also incredibly dumb. A total fuck knuckle.

- **Piss head** – *Kusipää*. A complete dumbass. Very low I.Q. Makes many of their friends and family members suffer due to their idiotic actions and bad decisions. An antonym of an outstanding member of society.

Cussing in Finnish

Cussing in Finland is a fine art indeed. Not only is it creative and foul, but it's also plentiful. It is said that Finns swear far more than their Nordic neighbors, reaching the same levels of prolific daily cussing as Scots and Russians. With that said, Finns don't just go cussing everywhere, in every situation, around everyone else. Just like in every other corner of the world, Finns don't generally cuss around strangers, in official situations or around children. So don't be the dickhead who belts out the only Finnish words they know - *"Vittu, Perkele, Saatana!"* (Cunt, Devil, Satan) as soon as they are introduced to a random Finn for the first time. This does not make you relatable or funny. In fact, it makes you a rude and ignorant cunt head. Have some manners for fucks sake, wait until you know the Finn in question for a bit, and maybe after a while you can reveal your linguistic skills.

The most common cuss words in Finnish are similar to the ones in other countries: body parts, bodily fluids and so on. However, the way they get paired up with other words, as well as how the word is used when spoken, is quite unique.

- **Cunt** - *Vittu.* This is used in a similar fashion as 'fuck' in English speaking countries. We could leave it at this, but there's so much more to *Vittu* than that.

Vittu is the mother of all cuss words in the Finnish language, its true meaning *is* vagina after all. *Vittu* has sprouted its cuntly tentacles into many other forms of creative cussing and insulting your fellow man or woman, way past just the simple Cunt – *Vittu* – 'Fuck'. *Vittu* or more specifically *Vitun* can be placed in front of any word to emphasize the meaning, much like 'fucking'. As in 'fucking great' – *'vitun mahtava'*, but of course for Finns it reads 'Cunts great'. - 'Cunts big' – *Vitun iso* – 'Cunts stupid' – *Vitun tyhmä*.

- **Spring of cunts and a returning winter of cocks** - *Vittujen kevät ja kyrpien takatalvi.* This simply means: 'Damned', but is much more fun to say. If you are not quite up to spurting out such a long phrase for a simple 'damned', feel free to use the shorter version of this:

- **Spring of Cunts**. – *Vittujen kevät.* It gets the job done just the same.

- **Cunting** - *Vittuilla.* This is a verb, derivative of the word *vittu*, and means 'talking shit to your face' or 'making fun of you in a mean and sarcastic way, to your face' – or just trying to piss you off. This often happens when people are under the influence of alcohol and can easily lead into a bar stool in your face type of situation. Avoid cunting if at all possible.

Back at the bar

Pirkko: "That guy over there told me my outfit looks nice, but I wasn't sure if he was serious or if he was just cunting."

Raija: "Probably serious, you do look stunning tonight. Sequins was a good call."

Pirkko: "Aww, thanks Raija! Well just in case, I told him to smell shit. You can never be too sure with these dickheads."

- **Cunted Off** – *Vituttaa*. This verb means being pissed off or upset. A feeling of 'fucked offness' if you will.

- **Cunts / Cunts is** – *Vitut/Vitut on*. This simply means 'no' – Or rather: 'NO!' A sure sign of not agreeing with you, at all. As in: 'You are dead wrong and a total dipshit on top of that.'

- **Cunt like / Cunty** – *Vittumainen*. This adjective is used to describe a mean or evil person. Someone who will hurt you on purpose and then laugh about it later, a real cunt-like fellow.

- **Cunt yeah** – *Vittu joo*. Used in a same way as 'fuck yeah'.

Boys and their toys

Mikko: "Hey Pekka, take a look at my new motorcycle. It's at least three times faster than the piece of junk you are riding."

Pekka: "Cunts is! I will race you, and your shit bike anytime and win easily. God Mikko, you are such a cunt head."

Mikko: "Smell a cunt. You know mine is faster. Hey do you want to go get some sausage fries from the kiosk? I'm getting hungry."

Pekka: "Cunt yeah. I'm starving."

- **Shit** – *Paska.* Needs no explanation. Used in the same way as shit everywhere. It can be used to describe actual shit, a person, an object, a situation, a job, a quality, or pretty much anything. Very useful and versatile combination of four letters, or five if you are conversing in Finnish.

- **Ass** – *Perse.* Ass is an ass, no matter where you are at.

- **Eat ass** – *Syö perse.* This is fighting words right here. A crude insult that should not be taken lightly.

- **Pulling asses over your shoulder** – *Vetää perseet olalle*. This means 'getting drunk', thoroughly shit faced, intentionally intoxicated.

- **Piss** – *Kusi*. Literal meaning 'urine' and in this form is rarely used to mean anything else. However, there are few derivatives from this word that are worth mentioning.

- **Pissing/taking a piss** – *Kusettaa*. This has nothing to do with the act of urinating, but rather 'lying' or 'cheating' – similar to American 'bullshitting.' Only used in the verb form though, never in a way that the word 'bullshit' is used to describe something that is not true.

- **Piss in a sock** – *Kusi sukassa*. This means you are very scared or downright terrified.

- **Being in piss** – *Olla kusessa*. This means you are in big trouble. Similar to 'being in deep shit' in America.

- **We are in piss, but we'll swim** – *Kusessa ollaan, mutta uidaan*. Yet another perfect example of the Finnish way of persevering and looking on the bright side. Never give up, even if you are in trouble, you just keep going. Even if you have to swim in urine.

Boys on the road

Pekka: "Dude! I think we just drove past a speed trap!"

Mikko: "Spring of cunts! Are you sure?! Oh wait, are you pissing me?"

Pekka: "Haha! You should have seen your face. You had piss in a sock so bad."

Mikko: "Smell a cunt piss head."

- **Hell** – *Helvetti.* Used much in the same way as "Hell" elsewhere: 'Why in the hell' - *Miksi helvetissä* – 'Where in the hell' – *Missä helvetissä* - 'Oh hell'. – *Voi helvetti* or just plain *Helvetti!* - Hell! However, the exception is made when using it to describe something disgusting, as in:

- **Yuck Hell** - *Hyi Helvetti.* A great way of expressing your utter distaste to whatever grossness is in front of you. 'Yuck Hell' is typically accompanied by a visible shudder.

- **Perkele/Devil** – *Perkele.* Perkele is another name for the ancient Finnish pagan god Ukko, the god of thunder and rain, similar to Thor in Norse mythology. When the first Bible was printed in Finnish, the word Devil was replaced with Perkele, making it a sin to utter such a word. We believe this was in an effort of trying to deter Finns from speaking of their old gods and getting used to the new one. But as Finns of the past didn't give a damn, they kept saying the name of their old god *Perkele*, be it in a curse or a prayer, it didn't much matter, but the word definitely stuck. Despite its godly history, make no mistake, this is considered to be one of the most powerful cuss words in the Finnish language.

- **Satan** – *Saatana*. Often used cuss word with biblical history, but turned into profanity in everyday language. Similar in use to 'God Damned'

- **God help** – *Jumalauta*. In today's society, this does not mean you are asking for help from God, if anything you are cursing them. This is a combination of the words *Jumala* (God) and *Auta* (Help) omitting one of the a's in the middle. When translated, its meaning is closer to 'God Damned' than 'God Help' and it is definitely a profanity and not a cry for help.

- **Oh ass brush** – *Voi perseensuti*. This is used in the way 'dammit' would be used, when something does not go quite as planned. We have not been able to find the origin story of this saying, or what the said 'ass brush' actually was, or what it was used for, but it is a delightful little curse nevertheless and definitely worth using.

- **Oh jays eggs/Oh jays dick** – *Voi närhen munat.* – *Muna* in Finnish means both an egg and a penis. This fact lends itself to countless opportunities of cheeky ways of slipping a penis into a benign conversation and it is no surprise that this is exploited widely. This particular saying will express mild frustration and could be interpreted to mean eggs since we are talking about a bird. However, we find this is a rather generous interpretation, and as far as we are concerned, the meaning is on the phallic side.

- **Oh goats wiener** – *Voi kilin kikkelit.* – Expresses mild frustration, similar to 'Damn'. Another golden phrase that has roots in Finland's rich agricultural past.

- **Oh goats cunt** – *Voi kilin vittu.* A stronger version of the above, expressing extreme frustration. Used when plain 'cunt' seems unnecessarily harsh and you want to mix some animal action and whimsy into your expressive language.

- **Oh the chicken cage of horror** – *Voi kauhistuksen kanahäkki.* – This is an interesting one, and once again the origin of this saying is unknown to us. It can be used in place of 'Oh my God' – when something is gross, messed up or takes you by total surprise, or if you just pretend to be horrified when seeing your

68

kids room, trying to drive home a point that they need to get off their phones and clean the place.

- **Oh good mosquitos** – *Voi hyvät hyttyset*. This is used in the way 'oh my goodness' is used in English speaking countries.

- **May the hell ring** – *Hitto/Helvetti soikoon*. This is used in a same way than 'darn it' is used in America.

- **Oh tallow candles of heaven** – *Voi taivahan talikynttilät*. This is also used in the way 'oh my goodness' is used elsewhere, but is viewed as somewhat of an old-fashioned curse, something your grandmother might say. A good one to know if you work or reside in an old home.

Maija's bilberry picking trip

Pirkko:	"Did you hear that Maija was attacked by a bear on Shit Hill last week!"
Raija:	"Oh tallow candles of heaven! Is she ok?"
Pirkko:	"She is ok, just a bit scratched up. We were on Shit Hill just last week. It could have been us."
Raija:	"Oh good mosquitos! That's scary."

Literal language

Finnish is said to be one of the most difficult languages to learn and we have all seen the grammar comparison memes depicting the Finnish grammar to be the biggest beast in the world. That may be true when it comes to grammar, and all of those ungodly word endings one is supposed to know how to use correctly, but there are a great many things about the Finnish language, that make it easier to learn than many other languages, not to mention the funniest one around.

Finnish language is a very phonetic language, much like Esperanto where each letter is always pronounced, and always pronounced the same exact way. There are no sight words, and there are no silent letters. If you know your alphabet, you know how to spell each, and every Finnish word, just by sounding it out.

Many of the Finnish words are very literal and easy to figure out, even if you have not heard that particular word before. Finns like to combine words which make them longer, almost like putting beads on a string. Some of the words are admittedly long, and were probably made up just to show off. Take "Lentokonesuihkuturbiinimoottoriapumekaanikkoaliup-seerioppilas" for example. This glorious word means: Airplane jet turbine engine auxiliary mechanic non-commissioned officer student. Ridiculous, we know.

A small sampling of literal Finnish words

Knowledge Machine – *Tietokone* – Computer

Knowledge Base - *Tietokanta* - Database

Knowledge Protection – *Tietosuoja* – Data protection

Body/Corps Room – *Ruumishuone* - Morgue

Body/Corps Chest – *Ruumisarkku* – Coffin

Body/Corps Car – *Ruumisauto* – Hearse

Load Car – *Kuorma-auto* – Truck

Route/Line Car – *Linja-auto* – Bus

Pedal Wheel – *Polkupyörä* – Bicycle

Motor Wheel – *Moottiripyörä* - Motorcycle

Motor Sleigh – *Moottorikelkka* – Snowmobile

Own Home House – *Omakotitalo* – Single Family House

Story/Floor House – *Kerrostalo* – Apartment block

Iron Road – *Rautatie* – Railway

Earth Road – *Maantie* – Highway

Breast Vest – *Rintaliivit* - Bra

Sock Pants – *Sukkahousut* - Tights

Running Rug – *Juoksumatto* - Treadmill

Shield Toad – *Kilpikonna* – Turtle

Christmas Goat – *Joulupukki* – Santa Claus

Salmon Snake – *Lohikäärme* - Dragon

Ice Cupboard – *Jääkaappi* – Refrigerator

Power Mixer – *Tehosekoitin* - Blender

Coffee Boiler – *Kahvinkeitin* – Coffeemaker

Dust Sucker – *Pölynimuri* – Vacuum cleaner

Car Stable – *Autotalli* – Garage

Sea Hedgehog – *Merisiili* – Sea urchin

Money Bag – *Rahapussi* - Wallet

Stream Horse – *Virtahepo* – Hippopotamus

Live Picture Theatre – *Elokuvateatteri* – Movie Theater

Animal Garden – *Eläintarha* – Zoo

Children's Garden – *Lastentarha* – Day care

Tree Garden – *Puutarha* – Garden (even if it has no trees)

Plant Land – Kasvimaa – Vegetable garden

Heart Doctor – *Sydänlääkäri* - Cardiologist

Skin Doctor – *Iholääkäri* – Dermatologist

Cancer Doctor – *Syöpälääkäri* - Oncoligist

Children's Doctor – *Lastenlääkäri* - Pediatrician

Gynecologist – *Gynekologi* - Gynecologist

– and you thought this last one was going to be something naughty. Shame on you, Finns are not savages after all. At least not when their legs are high up in the stirrups.

Gardening

Pirkko:	"Wow Raija, your plant land looks amazing!"
Raija:	"Thanks! I found some great gardening ideas in my knowledge machine.
Pirkko:	"Isn't internet great? Last year I bought slightly used running rug online for 50 euros."
Raija:	"What a find! A lot easier on the old money bag than buying one from the sport store."
Pirkko:	"Although, now it just takes up space in my car stable. Do you want a running rug for 50 euros?"

Finnish Summer Sports

Like most things in life, Finns have found their very own way to do competitions. Finns are by nature extremely competitive and can make anything into a competitive sport. While they embrace some of the more mainstream sports and pastimes such as soccer and hockey, many other sports and activities only exist in the land of the 3 million saunas, and 490 Shit Ponds. Let's not forget about the Shit Ponds.

Wife Carrying World Championship Competition

Eukonkannon MM-kilpailut

This is probably the most famous of authentic Finnish sports. Its roots are deep in Finnish history, probably in the medieval times, when maidens were regularly stolen to be wives. The race course is a 253.5 meter, or 831.69 feet obstacle course, that a man must complete, while carrying his wife on his back. The lady in question does not actually have to be his wife, any random woman will do, as long as they weigh at least 49 kg / 108 lbs. The obstacle course starts with a short run leading into a chest deep pool. This is followed by a waist-high log one needs to go over, then a 50-meter dash followed by another log and another dash into the finish line. The fastest man wins their wives weight in beer. Finns have held World Championship Competitions in Wife Carrying each year in Sonkajärvi since 1992 and each year the crowds and the number of contestants gets larger as the competition gains in popularity.

Rubber Boot Throwing Championships

Saappaanheiton SM-kilpailut

World championships in Rubber Boot Throwing started in Finland in 1992. As the word got around, this competition has moved onto a bigger arena. Besides Finland, the World Championships have been held in Sweden, Estonia, Italy, Germany and Poland. Finland still has Nationals each year, where the team of the very best boot throwers is selected to represent Finland in the World Championships. The sport is very similar to the discus throw, but instead of a metal disc, you throw a rubber boot.

Stick Horse Riding competition – Hobby Horsing

Keppihevoskilpailut

This is competitive riding, just like on a real horse, only you ride a stick horse. People spend a lot of time and money making their stick horse the best in show, as well as practicing their perfect gallop, trot and stride. This competition is professionally judged and extremely competitive on a national level, with Hobby Horse organizations located in towns across the country. National Hobby Horsing competitions reach a wide audience and the tickets to these events are available in advance or at the door. As the sport has grown, it has also attracted the healthy support of some big-name sponsors. This is a nice option for the equestrian lovers who don't have the slightest desire to spend their days shoveling manure and spending their money on vet bills and expensive riding gear.

Swamp Soccer World Championships

Suopotkupallon MM-kilpailut

Swamp soccer is exactly what it sounds like. You play soccer running knee deep in a swamp. Everyone gets dirty and the workout you get from this sport is tenfold to what you would get playing the same game on a well maintained green. This is considered to be soccer for the total bad asses and the championship is highly coveted. The first National Swamp Soccer competition was held in 1998. Around 200 teams from around the globe compete in the Swamp Soccer World Championship Tournament annually.

Cell Phone Throwing Competition

Kännykänheiton MM-Kilpailut

The first Cell Phone Throwing World Championship was organized in 2000. It is held each summer in Savonlinna and contestants are coming from all corners of the world. Although the competition originated in Finland and the championship has always gone to a Finn, smaller competitions have started popping up around Europe. Now Norway, Switzerland, Germany, Holland and Belgium have their own Cell Phone Throwing Championships as well. The record throw has stood since 2005, at 94.97 meters.

Air Guitar World Championship Competition

Ilmakitarasoiton MM-kisat

This competition with imaginary instruments has been held annually in Oulu since 1996. It is possibly one of the most internationally known Finnish summer competitions. Over the years this event has spread across the globe and air guitar semifinals are now held in over 20 different countries. With lasers, big screens and huge crowds, this competition definitely has entertainment value for anyone with a pulse. The judges will rate contestants in: stage presence, mimesmanship and airness or the artfulness of the performance.

Funny Finnish foods

Finns have developed very special taste buds over the centuries of living in isolation and doing the daily surviving thing. The main staple of the Finnish diet is **Rye Bread** - *Ruisleipä*. So much so that the local McDonalds has developed a Ruis Feast hamburger replacing the traditional bun with a dark rye flat bread. Rye – *Ruis* – makes a very dark, sour and hard bread, that due to its dryness, can be stored without it spoiling for a very long time. In the olden days, breads were baked only a few times a year, and hung out on long rods across the main living space in people's houses. It takes a while to develop the taste for this type of bread, but once you learn to love it, you will likely crave it for the rest of your days.

Blood has always been used in Finnish cooking in variety of ways. You can find beef blood sold in pint size plastic bottles in stores across the country. To a Finn, there is nothing strange about this. It is used to make sausages and even the world-famous **Blood Pancakes** - *Veriletut*, which by the way, was part of the regular school menu for decades and in some parts of the country may still be on the menu. If you are not keen on making bloody pancakes from scratch, blood pancakes can be purchased ready made in any grocery store. Blood pancakes with lingonberry jam are definitely something every visitor in Finland should try. Vampire or not, your body will love the iron boost it gets from this delicious treat.

Karelian Pies - *Karjalanpiirakat* are originally from the eastern part of the Finland, but over the years they have spread across the entire country. These pies are typically made of a rye and wheat mixed crust and have either mashed potato or, more commonly, a sticky rice pudding filling. Once the piece of well flattened dough is filled with the desired filling, the edges are folded on top of the filling and wrinkled, making a somewhat of a vagina-shaped pie. Hence the nickname *Pimppipiirakka* – Cooch pie. It is often joked about that each baker makes the pies a little different, as if modeling the pies after their own furburger. A baker's signature of sorts. Cooch jokes aside, these pies are delicious and are typically enjoyed with egg butter mix spread over the top. Egg butter in Finnish is called *munavoi* – which can be translated as 'Egg Butter' or 'Dick Butter' depending on which *Muna* you are currently thinking about. So be a Finn for a day and have your vagina pie with dick butter, we know you will love it.

Mämmi is a curious mixture of water, malt, rye flour, syrup and bitter orange peel. There is no translatable word that we know of, and the word *Mämmi* does not mean anything, aside from this pitch-black grainy textured porridge like dish, that looks like straight up feces. *Mämmi* is a delicacy that mostly appeals to the older generation, much like lutefisk, and is only available in stores during the Easter season. Thank goodness for that, as in our humble opinion, it tastes much like it looks like; crap. So much so, that *Mämmi* could probably be used to fool a dung beetle into rolling it into a neat little ball.

Liver casserole – *maksalaatikko*. Another gem from the school menu, and the frozen section of your neighborhood grocery. It is exactly as it sounds, a casserole made of ground up beef or pork liver, rice, milk, eggs, onion, raisins, syrup, and spices. Just like blood pancakes, liver casserole is enjoyed with lingonberry jam. Mmmmm.

Spreadable Reindeer Cheese – *Porosulatejuusto*. This cheese can be slightly misleading, as it is not made out of reindeer milk. This tasty spreadable cheese is made of cow's milk and infused with small bits of smoked reindeer meat, making it a perfect all-in-one spread for your sandwich.

Sausage - *Makkara* is another tried and true staple of the Finnish diet. Along with beer and rye bread, sausages are sold like hot cakes around the country, especially during the summer months when people retreat to their summer cottages. Most Finnish sausages have a very smooth texture and lack the mysterious lumps of meat like products which never fail to surprise a sausage chewer in mid bite in other countries. Due to its obviously phallic shape and similar size, Finnish sausage has earned the nickname of *Lerssin pätkä* – **'piece of schlong'**. If that does not make you want to stuff your face with it, nothing will.

It's an onion!

Sillä sipuli - That's a wrap. Congratulations! You are now fully equipped to immerse yourself into the Finnish culture, lightyears ahead of any expat or visitor that has not yet read this book. So, go ahead, book your ticket to HEL - (Yes, this is the official abbreviation for the Helsinki airport) and enjoy this northern wonderland of 'Shit Ponds' and 'Vagina Pies' to its full capacity. Seriously, you should. But probably not in November, unless of course, you are a total badass and have a habit of showing off. November is notorious for its coldness, wetness and its soul crushing darkness. Or perhaps you really are a vampire and are already drooling at the chance to buy blood in pint-sized bottles at any grocery store and love the idea of spending months in almost complete darkness with little-to-no sunlight. Then November will be perfect for you, and Finland does not judge. They will welcome you with open arms, regardless of your mystical status. But once the snow arrives, Finnish winter, is nothing short of magical. Book your winter vacation to Lapland and stay in a glass igloo, fall asleep while watching the northern lights up above. Visit Kuusamo and take your snow shoes up the Fart Hill. You won't regret it.

But if you are not an undead bloodsucker who doesn't feel cold, or a winter sports enthusiast, summer is definitely the best time to plan your trip. This is a perfect time to enjoy the incredible richness of Finnish nature. You will be amazed at the greenness and the millions upon millions of wildflowers that rush to bloom in every nook and cranny during the sunny summer months. With thousands of forests, lakes, rivers and islands in the middle of the most beautiful and pristine nature, Finland will give you the outdoor experience of a life time. Or perhaps you are an athlete and competitive wife carrying piqued your interest. Grab your lady and fly her up to the most unique sporting event on the planet. If culture is your thing, Finland has a mind-blowing art scene, as well as a plethora of museums for a culture hungry visitor to enjoy. For the musically inclined, Finland has summer festivals coming out the wazoo, including but not limited to Rock, Heavy Metal, Opera, Jazz and Tango festivals. And of course, the Air Guitar World Championships in Oulu. Whatever your flavor, we are confident that Finland will have something up her sleeve that you will love to experience!

In the end

the thanks is standing

In the end, the thanks is standing/erected - *Lopussa Kiitos Seisoo*. This is a common saying that perfectly describes the rewards for a job well done. In the end, you will get the thanks, in the form of a traditional 'Thank you' from someone else, or from within. It's that warm feeling inside, when you know that you did it and you can be proud of yourself!

Writing this book has been so much fun and we hope you enjoy reading it as much as we enjoyed writing it. Heartfelt thanks to our panel of experts, you know who you are, and all the amazing people who supported this idea, or rather, demanded this book to be written.

The thanks that are erected in the end, are for you!